Dominate Your Niche

Ideas on How to Beat Competition and Increase Your Site's Traffic

By: Jeff Moore

9781635014419

PUBLISHERS NOTES

Disclaimer – Speedy Publishing LLC

Speedy Publishing LLC

40 E Main Street, Newark, Delaware, 19711

Contact Us: 1-888-248-4521

Website: http://www.speedypublishing.co

REPRINTED Paperback Edition: 9781635014419:

Manufactured in the United States of America

Dedication

To Anthony. Thanks for the inspiration, my little man.

TABLE OF CONTENTS

Chapter 1- The Secrets to Increasing Website Traffic 5

Chapter 2- Reach Out to Your Market...................................10

Chapter 3- Hire Professionals to Help You 17

Chapter 4- It's OK to Copy But Not Plagiarize 22

Chapter 5- Free Is Attractive 26

Chapter 6- Don't Just Build Your Brand, Build It Right.................30

Chapter 7- Do Things Right..34

Chapter 8- Some Quick Guidelines on Blogging 39

Chapter 9- When Does the BIG Traffic Come?...................44

Chapter 10- BONUS! Free Tips on Converting Traffic to Buying
Customers 51

About The Author...61

CHAPTER 1- THE SECRETS TO INCREASING WEBSITE TRAFFIC

The World Wide Web has truly pervaded all aspects of human existence. Everything and everyone is going online now, and the move towards a totally connected world is not "if" anymore, it's "when".

Statistics show that up to 85% of the people who spend time online also purchase online. If you take the North American continent alone where more than 75% of the population have a broadband Internet connection at home, even if a fraction of these people buy online, it is still a huge market.

Online purchasing is also seeing tremendous growth and many companies are projecting a doubling of volume in just three years.

If you take PayPal as a case in point, they have gone from $2 billion in payment volumes in 2002 to $16 billion in 2009 with revenues crossing $2.4 billion.

Amazon is another case that you can take as an example. Considering that Amazon is one of the largest online retailers, if not the largest, just looking at their total sales volume will show you that the trend in terms of online purchasing is only going up. While just a few years ago, in 2006, Amazon was about par with retail sales, since then they have posted higher growth rates, including during the recession years while retail sales has seen a steady decline in sales. Amazon has posted a 16% growth since the last one year alone while retail sales have grown only by 2.5%.

Online is where you will have to be in the future and whether you are selling something or just blogging about your thoughts, if you are serious about it you will have to do something to increase web traffic to your site.

There are a number of ways in which you can do this and there are a number of people who give free advice on what you need to do to increase web traffic. One of the most common things you hear is SEO or Search Engine Optimization, and while this is something that you have to keep in mind, there are a number of other things that you can also think about.

This guide is meant to be informative to help beginners who want to set up their own websites on the salient points that they will have to keep in mind while they do this. Some of the tips may be a little complicated, but most of them are very simple and how popular your site becomes depends on how effectively you can bring them all together.

Your Site's Content Drives Traffic

The content that you put up on your website is the most critical thing that you need to think of. In the same way that a store will do well only if they sell things that people need, you will get people visiting your website only if you give something that people are looking for. Of course it also means that you are entering a crowded market because genuinely unique niches are hard to come by. If you do find one, you are on to a good thing, but even if not, as long as you make the content appealing, you are sure to find takers.

Do something that others don't do. For example, selling products or services online is catching on really fast, and you will find a number of sites with products that link back to the larger online retailers like Amazon or eBay. If you want to do the same, it is not that difficult, except that there is something that you will have to give that other websites do not offer. For example, if you offer a personal review of the product that you are selling you are sure to develop a certain number of loyal customers and as long as the reviews are informative and helpful you will only get more customers with time.

There are other websites that offer the same thing, but most of them will have only a couple of lines that they probably found in other websites and copied. If you give information that is more detailed and specific, things that only a user would know, you are sure to make a hit.

Give Reasons for People to Come Back – OFTEN!

This does take more work and time, but unless you are willing to invest in good content, there is really no point in proceeding further. Make sure that you do your research. Even if you are only selling dog collars, as long as you give the pros and cons of each one honestly people will appreciate it. The goal should be to make the content such that people who even casually visit your site once will bookmark it and keep coming back.

KISS Your Way up to Number 1

While writing your content, remember that just because you want to be informative you should not have long winded articles. Statistics show that between 600 and 800 words is the best length for most online articles. If you want to fill space in your site use other interactive content. Not only will this make the whole thing nicer to see and read it will also relieve the monotony of just plain text.

Even if you do not have the expertise to create interactive content, just using bullet points and charts in-between text will break it up into smaller more easily read pieces.

Be True to Yourself

Lastly, while writing, never lose your human voice. While writing it is easy to lose the personal touch that you give when talking and instead go for a more professional voice. The only thing that this will serve to do is to make visitors feel unwanted.

This becomes more of a problem as you grow, because as you see more money come in you will start to streamline the content. You need to walk a tight rope here because it is very easy to lose what brought people to your site in the first place while doing this. The risk of changing anything is that just as there is potential for success, there is an equally good chance for failure too.

Jeff Moore

One more thing that you should keep in mind when developing web content is that the more graphics you have, the more time it takes to load the page. While this may not be a problem with many people because they have a broadband connection, a number of people access the net through their phones and tablets, and heavy websites really slow down these machines when not on a Wi-Fi connection. Find that balance.

Chapter 2- Reach Out to Your Market

Newsletters and subscribers are a big thing in many websites nowadays. Websites ask people to subscribe to their free newsletters and keep sending out information every week or sometimes more frequently depending on the strategy that they follow. A few years ago, there may have been an issue with spam filters and emails being placed in junk folders. Today, this is still true but ISP are realizing the fact that news letters are here to stay, so place newsletters and email info high on your list of to do's when feeding your subscribers.

When you do send out your emails and newsletters it is a good idea to get creative with content and the title of your email. Interesting titles create open rates, and open rates create revenue. Try to offer interesting titles which offer value. Depending on your business you should be able to work out what your subscribers want to read and what sells after some time of research.

Provide Options

A better idea is to give the option to people to subscribe to an RSS feed. This gives them the option to either choose to subscribe or not which means that only genuinely interested people will. It will also give you a much more accurate idea of how popular your site is because most of those who subscribe will actually read what you have to say. You now have three good options for people to read your content.

1. RSS Feed

2. Email Newsletters

3. Your website content via bookmarks

Give Value

When you have your subscriber interest, the best ways of generating interest is to give huge value. Don't just write rehashed information that is easily found in other places online. If you are recommending a particular software for a specific purpose gives honest impressions that are not found elsewhere. You may think that this is too much to give away freely, but look at it this way. Open Source is catching on like blazes now, and there is a free alternative to almost everything, including Operating Systems. If you want to charge for your opinions as well as for the product that you sell, you will find that someone else is only charging for the product and is offering their opinions freely resulting in a movement away from your site.

In conclusion to giving value, ensure you give the best value. Remember, you are in competition with a lot of other websites and newsletters around the globe. Stand out to make a difference.

Be a Member of the Community

If you are starting a website business, chances are that there is already an online community on the niche that you want to start yours in. Make sure that you become involved and join them. Don't get so high and mighty that you think that everything that you write online should get you money. Write on other people's blogs and websites too. Just make sure that you link back to your site. Usually this is done in the signature and is one of the most effective ways of generating traffic to your site as long as what you write is worth reading. If the posting was good, people will come to your site just to read other articles written by you which is what you want. Gone are the times of selfish business owners. Giving and sharing content are the new ways to do business. People respect the knowledge of others and follow that knowledge. This is how you will generate your content.

Quote and Link

If you are pushed for content, another way is to quote from an article written elsewhere on the net. Usually nobody minds you quoting as long as you give them credit for it and link back to their site as well. Not only is this good etiquette, it will also improve your standing within the community which means that slowly, other more established people will start to link to your site. Remember, people respect knowledge.

Apart from the traffic that this linking generates, there is another more valuable reason for doing this. Most search engines do not index a website as soon as it is hosted. There are a number of people who create sites on free to use communities and then do not follow it up. Obviously no search engine wants any site like this in their results. One way that they identify if a site is in use and is genuine is by the number of links back to it. If these links are from sites in good standing with the search engines, the chances of your site getting indexer faster are greater.

However, you do need to remember to write original content 99% of the time and do not quote everyone else's content 100% of the time. The search engines love original content.

Use Article Directories

An older, but still very popular way of getting these links back is by posting articles on article directories and then linking it to your site in the bio section. There are many such article directories that allow you to upload content free although they have certain criteria about the kind of articles that you can upload. E-zine Articles is only one among them and there are a number of others that you can post to.

What this does is help you upload a lot of content in places other than your website and then back link to your website thus improving your website standing with the search engines. This is where you use the SEO optimization that you hear about frequently. There are two goals to doing this, one is the already mentioned improving of ranking with search engines, and the other is that sometimes these articles will actually come up higher in the ranking than your site. If this happens you will be driving traffic to your site from there too. Remember, original content is always the best way to achieve the best rankings from your articles and your website content.

Not Everything Is a Marketing Opportunity

This is something that most people who have websites will have to do as a default. These online communities are where people meet and share information or just chat, all without moving from their chair. Whether you know it or not, just creating an ID in a community like Facebook or Twitter will ensure that you get some activity to your page. Even if there is nothing there to attract people, there may be people who just find your name appealing and visit your page.

Making sure that you devote time to having a good profile in these communities, and update them as to what is new is a good way of telling people about what you are doing. If you are in real earnest, you can be connected to hundreds, or thousands of people whom you hardly know, and if you can coax a portion of them to visit your site, you are once again driving that little more traffic your way.

Get to Know the Community

Before you start planning on using any community as a marketing tool, first know what they are. These places are just a virtual place where you can network with your friends, but the social etiquette remains. This means that just as you cannot go to your club and then start selling stuff there to your fellow club members; you cannot do that online either. Many people would be shocked to even consider doing something like this at their club, but will not think twice about approaching their network online.

Yet, unlike a club a networking site online gives you a number of facilities, the least of which is that you can inform your network about anything new in your life. Just as people would not take it badly if you sent out bulk messages that you have gotten married or have a child, you can inform people that you are starting a new venture. If worded properly you will receive replies wishing you the best in your new venture.

Be Natural, Don't Market

This is the last thing that you must do. Many people make this mistake and pay for it by not only not getting any increase in traffic, but by making sure that they have effectively alienated their network because they have just showed themselves to be someone who uses their personal network for business. Your Facebook or Twitter ID is where you post what is happening with you, not a place where you sell products or services; you do that in your website. For example, if you have a website that deals with cooking, and offer recipes, make sure that this is part of your ID. At a later date if you want to bring out a short book of recipes for a price that you hope to sell online as an eBook, just telling your network about it will give you a lot of dividends. Don't approach them telling them that you hope that they will support your new venture by buying what you are selling, that is the worst thing that you can do.

Instead treat them as you would your friends. Just keep them informed about what's happening with your life, and that this is a big thing with you. If you don't push your product, you will be prompting people to at least visit your site to take a look at what you have to offer. As to whether they buy your book or not depends a lot on other factors the least of them being that the book should have some real stuff that they cannot find for free elsewhere.

But even if your book does not sell, you have done something else, and that is to drive traffic to your site and the bottom line is that even if one income stream, you hoping to make money out of the book, does not click, you will probably make some out of your advertisers because of the increased traffic.

CHAPTER 3- HIRE PROFESSIONALS TO HELP YOU

This is easier said than done, but using experts is one of the most effective ways of generating traffic to your site. Whatever niche you are in, unless you yourself are an expert, getting one to write articles for you is a good idea. Of course, not many experts will actually consent to write anything for you, which is where the previous point comes in. Most of these experts would be high standing members of the community and as long as you lay the groundwork properly and get connected, they are sure to notice you. Over time you can approach them about writing something for you, and even if they decline, you've not lost anything by asking. By becoming a respected member in the community you will just be making it that much harder for them to refuse you when you do ask.

This is not something that you can do a couple of weeks after you start, or even a couple of months after you do. It takes time to earn a name, and even if you are not considered an expert in the field, as long as you make sure that you are a respected member in the community your chances are greater. Once you have an established website which offers some good content and has a reputable name, guest writers will come naturally. People will want to write for you, because of your search engine standings and traffic rankings. You more you grow the more attention you will get from interested writers and invited writers.

For example, if you want to start a website that recommends/sells software, make sure that you join a community where such software is discussed. Join as many as you can, and make sure that you participate. Help out others who ask for help and if you do this long enough it is the best way to get noticed. If you offer your time and expertise for free not only will those you helped directly come to your site the next time they want something, other members in your community will also link to your articles. Over time, some of them may even start recommending that their visitors visit your site. Helping others very rarely does not pay; it just takes time for you to see the results.

Let Google Help

• Google Analytics

Any business revolves around metrics. You need details of how many people visit your site, how long they spend at your site, which pages are the most often viewed and many other details that will help you improve your site. There are a few different ways to do this.

The most popular way is to use Google analytics. Google analytics is a free code that Google gives you that you have to put into each page of your website. This code runs every time a person visits your website and keeps track of everything from whether this was their first visit to how long they spend in each page. This is not a foolproof method because this system does not take into account people, who disable Java script in their browsers, but the number of people who do this is very small and in any case Google only uses 500,000 randomly taken hits for their metrics.

Although Google analytics is the largest used such software there are others too that you can use, both free as well as paid. There are issues with running such software starting with increased loading time, but they are getting better and better with each passing month.

There are some websites that do not use Google analytics because the information thus collected can be accessed by others. By others, it does not mean retail customers, but for example Google itself retains this information for their uses. Large corporations are not comfortable with other companies gaining information about their websites and therefore do not go with Google, but for most of us analytics is good enough and an excellent resource for small to medium business owners.

• Keyword Tool

Using key words is one of the most important things that you will have to do. First, you will have to decide what the keywords are that most people may use when they want to look for what you are providing. Think about the words people would use to find your site, and the more people who contribute, the more exhaustive the list is going to be. After you have narrowed down the general keywords that you think that people will be looking for, you can use specific software like Google's keyword tool, Yahoo's Overture Keyword selector tool, Wordtracker, Keyword Dictionary, Market Samurai or any other tool that you are comfortable with.

Most of them are free to use and will give you a combination of keywords based on the keyword that you typed in. This will help you identify the best combination of keywords to use in your content because it will give you the search strings that are the most commonly used in relation to the word you typed in.

Be Dynamic, Not Static

This does not mean that once you write and post your articles you are finished. Keywords are very dynamic, and often, along with trends the search strings that are often used too often will change. You do not have to necessarily change the entire content in your site during times like this. Just making sure that you incorporate the new keywords is sometimes good enough. Remember, reviving old content is a great way to keep your content highly ranked.

Don't Overdo It

This may sound simple but in reality it is not. This is because you will have to walk a fine line between over-stuffing your articles with different keywords and with putting in too few. And even then most search engines are able to identify if the keywords come logically as part of the sentence or have been forced in somewhere where they are not suitable.

Nobody knows exactly how the search engines do this as it is their trade secret, but suffice it to say that just because your article is full of keywords it does not necessarily mean that the site is going to get a better ranking. Often an article with the keyword appearing just once will pop up higher than one where it has been repeated a number of times. Keep this in mind when writing your articles; don't overdo it with the same key words. Google likes to read content like a reader, not a manufactured key word hungry robot.

Jeff Moore

Also never copy content, unless you are linking back to where you are copying from. All search engines are able to identify copied content and if it finds that your article is copied, you will even lose ranking because it will tend to push your site to the bottom of the pile. Original content is always the best way to rank. Don't forget this.

Chapter 4- It's OK to Copy But Not Plagiarize

This may sound a little odd, especially after the previous chapter but this is something that everyone does. You don't copy the content; instead you copy what someone else is doing better by getting more traffic to their website. You will know what websites are getting more traffic to them by their ranking on search engines. You can also use Alexa.com to check the rankings of websites you are interested in.

Do Your Groundwork

This is not as easy as you would think though. You will first have to locate all the sites that are the leaders in the segment you are in. There are a number of tools that will help you do this, and Google

PageRank is both very useful as well as free and can be installed in any browser.

After you form your list you will have to visit each of these sites and figure out for yourself why they are doing better than you. Check different search engines that will give you this information and this is where your true talent lies. The more accurate you are in identifying why others do well, the better you can make your site.

While making changes you will obviously have to continue tracking hits to your site, but do not be hasty and make changes quickly. It will take a day for the changes to be indexed properly in the search engines, and even then you will have to allow some time before the changes start making any difference. It is a slow process and you learn as you go.

Never directly copy website content, this is not only illegal but detrimental to your website search engine rankings. Remember no one - not even Google - likes a copycat. Use content as ideas to create your own content and make it better.

Focus on What Works for Others

Many people do not realize it when they start out, but it is difficult to start a website and put in information that is always appealing. To most of us as long as the article that we post is well written and interesting to read, it should work, but it rarely does. You need to know which portion of your website is working well and which is not.

You can get this information using Google analytics, and once you identify this trend, it is up to you to start concentrating on that portion of your website. For all you know the portion of your website that you would think is the least appealing will get the most number of look ins.

For example, if you have started a website where you post reviews of different home appliances and also sell them, your assumption would be that the most hits would be on the reviews. When looking at the metrics however you may be surprised to find that it is your blog or your comments page that is receiving the most hits.

What you should immediately do is to concentrate on the comments page and leverage it. Ultimately advertisers look at the total number of hits on your website. So as long as you can maintain a consistent number of visits a day or week, you should be doing well.

Of course it means that you will probably need to rework your review page so that it too starts seeing more traffic, but that should be the second thing on your priority, not first.

Be Patient

Many websites that are really popular have a ratio of around 1:20. This means that for every 20 articles that you put in, one will turn out popular. For beginners this ratio will be much higher, but keep plugging away at it. Nobody finds a winning combination instantly and you should be willing to spend a lot of time on making your website a success. Don't be afraid to try out new things. If it does not work you can always remove the page later, but if it does click, you have something on which you can concentrate on.

Another thing that you should not worry too much about is not so much the number of hits on your website, but on how long the people stay. There are a number of reasons why people may just open your site and close it immediately. Those who matter are the ones who stay for a certain length of time. Although, for most commercial purposes it is the number of hits on your page that matter, for you to develop a good site it is the people who stay on whom you will have to concentrate on. Only then will you know what people are visiting your site for and provide more of the same. Google Analytics will provide all of these details for you.

CHAPTER 5- FREE IS ATTRACTIVE

This does not mean that you give out free products. It could very well be a simple eBook on a particular subject or free wallpaper.

For example, if you have a website that is related to IT you could give wallpapers or screen savers that you have designed. Many people do this, but not all ask for contact information as well. Remember we talked about building a list of contacts; well this is a way to do it. Exchange email addresses for content so you can add people to your newsletters and information distribution list.

You do not always have to ask for anything in exchange. There is fine line between giving items away for email addresses and becoming annoying to your visitors asking for some every time you give something away. Treat your readers and website visitors with respect. Give them freebies for simply being subscribers. This builds reputation. You can even ask them to share this on social media sites for the pleasure. These also build reputations and traffic.

Imagine you are opening a medical related site, giving out a short 10 or 20 page eBook on some ailment, say diabetes, will only do good. Of course if this book is not a good one you will be better off not offering it for free as the reputation that you will receive will be bad. If you give out an informative well written book, or really nice looking wallpaper, people will talk about your site and ultimately the amount of publicity generated will be greater than if you had spent 10 times as much as you did for what you gave away. By offer awesome value or basically something you could charge a fee for, people will love and share your content.

The traffic potential of giving away a free guide takes time, but the viral aspects and out of this world. The more shares and people you have reading and distributing your eBook, the more traffic you will get. Simple.

Advertise: It's Not Free but You Need It

Advertising will of course cost money, but you have no other way round. Any startup company needs marketing and even if it is online you will still have to market your wares. There are a number of innovative ways of doing this starting from fliers posted at different places to you having your website displayed prominently on your vehicle. Depending on the route you take the budget may be high or low and have varying degrees of effectiveness.

Go with AdSense

Not only offline but you can also go for online advertising. There are many websites that offer space to advertisers for a sum and you can advertise where you think you will get the maximum benefit. Pop ups, banners and advertisements are all popular, but the most popular is AdSense by Google. Anyone can sign up with AdSense and Google determines the kind of advertisements that go into the web-page.

If you want to advertise on other websites you must place a sealed bid for the space and if you are selected you can advertise. If you want to sell ad space, Google takes care of everything but takes a 32% cut in the income generated.

Even with this revenue loss it still makes sense to go with AdSense because a number of small operators who do not have the financial clout to do much have generated income from AdSense.

If you are purchasing ads, then the only thing that you are limited by is the budget you have. The more you have, the more you can advertise.

If you are looking at generating income through advertisements, you have to be a little careful about it. When your website is still new, and is not generating much traffic, many people will purchase ad space very cheap and then reap the benefit of all your hard work because they will be getting much more than what they paid for. It is better to wait a while until you get established before you start selling advertisements because of this.

Don't Get Too Greedy

Another bad thing and more important when it comes to generating traffic to the website is that a site that is covered with ads just turns people off. You may start to earn money quickly by adopting this strategy, but many browsers do not like sites that have a lot of advertisements meaning that you will actually be losing traffic by advertising, although this is one income stream that you cannot afford to ignore.

How you balance your need for income generation with your website is where your talent lies, and how well you do depends on how right you get it. There is really no simple rule that you can follow here. There are a number of sites that are loaded with ads and yet do well, while there are others that do not have too many and still do not do as well. There are a number of factors that are responsible, and only time will tell whether you are right in what you did or not.

CHAPTER 6- DON'T JUST BUILD YOUR BRAND, BUILD IT RIGHT

When you are developing your website, you need to have a vision of what you want from it. You are building up an organization, not just a website and the growth potential is limited only by your imagination. You need to establish a brand and live up to it.

Of course this takes time, but it is time well spent. You have to set expectations and make sure that you live up to them. If you are in the practice of putting in two posts a day, you will have to ensure that you continue to do so every day. You may complain that this means that you do not have any holidays or time off, and you will be right here. Yet, it will be worth it in the long run.

Statistics show that even if you miss one day the traffic falls immediately. Of course, if you are going to miss only one day this is not a long term impact, but if you are going to make a practice of doing this, you will start losing traffic instead of gaining it.

Plan Ahead

If you feel that you absolutely have to take a break, make sure that you plan in advance for it. There are a number of things you can do starting from outsourcing this blog posting to making sure that you have a ready supply of posts that you can post from anywhere. The whole world is connected these days and as long as you have already prepared the articles, all it is going to take is 10 or 15 minutes of your time to post it every day.

If you are putting in articles regularly, make sure that the quality of your work does not flag. With success don't become complacent. Outsource some of the more labor intensive work but make sure you check it for originality and quality. By staying on top of the work you choose to outsource your site will not lose the high standard that you want for your business.

Over time a certain website will stand for something, and you need to identify what this something is even before you start. Only then can you work towards it. If you just start without having any other goal than just that you want to earn money, there will be no direction to your site and it will vacillate here and there, never a good thing.

Use Meta Tags

If you have done a little bit of looking around before you started working on developing your website, you would have come across the term Meta tags. Many websites recommend that you use them when you develop your website. These Meta tags are nothing but HTML tags that are not visible on the page itself and are usually included inside the <HEAD> tag of the page.

Most of the advice will be towards you stuffing all your keywords within these tags. You can even put in keywords that do not occur within the body of the article itself. For example, if you are setting up a cooking website and plan on introducing various recipes and if one of the recipes have to do with making chicken dumplings, you can add this plus combinations of the same keyword like for example, good chicken dumplings, or best chicken dumplings or any other search string that you feel you want to add, but which may not necessarily sit well within the body of the article.

No to Keyword Stuffing

Unfortunately most search engines just ignore this tag and anything within. They started doing this nearly a decade back and nowadays even the use of this tag is highly debated in certain circles. The reason for this is because many web-masters started stuffing in keywords that did not have anything to do with their sites at all just to start directing more traffic there.

Anyway the bottom line is that if you use this tag to stuff in keywords you may even be doing yourself harm because some search engines actually penalize sites that do this.

Where Do I Use Meta Tags?

This does not mean that Meta tags are totally useless. Some search engines use what is inside the Meta tags coupled with what is within the articles to get a better idea of what the site contains. This is why the initial advice was to only include keywords that are related to what you are writing about.

Another thing that you can do is to put in a short description of what the site is about within this tag. If we take the same cooking website as an example, you could write a short one-liner like this

"A simple recipe to make chicken dumplings within 30 minutes". Usually this line would be incorporated to some extent in the summary that is given below your website in the search results page. This does not mean that all search engines will start to display what is within these tags but you at least have some amount of control over what is said about your site. Even Google that has come out a few years back and said that they ignore Meta tags, nowadays incorporate at least some amount of what is available in the Meta tags in their summary.

Other Uses

There are also other uses for Meta tags like if you do not want to index certain pages in your site, or if you do not want the search engines crawlers not to follow certain links in your site. Using Meta tags with the no index or no follow options will give you this. You may wonder why anyone would even want to not index their site, but there are cases when it is helpful. For example, if you have written an article on a certain subject, but over a few years you find that things have progressed and that this article may not be relevant any more, you have the option of removing that page, or archiving it. Unless you specify that you do not want this page indexed it will continue to show up on searches, and because it has been around far longer than the updated page will be higher in the rankings.

You can also use the tags to specify the content type, like if it is text or graphics, and the language used. Although this does not make that big a difference, it is really helpful, especially for those sites that offer a number of language options. The search engines will be better able to index each page separately, instead of taking everything to be duplicate content.

CHAPTER 7- DO THINGS RIGHT

- **Buy the Right Software**

If you have the money for it you can always outsource the development part of the website, but this is not the cheapest thing in the world to do. Of course, you can find freelancers who are willing to do the job cheaply, but then their concept of what you need and yours may be poles apart.

Like most businesses good website designers tend to charge more. This does not however mean that you should pay through your nose to get your website developed. There are a number of CMS tools that you can use to develop your own site. There is a whole hoard of software that you can use and each of them gives you different functionality.

You could go with online ones that allow you to develop and publish everything online, or you can go with applications that allow you to develop your site locally and then publish it online. You get both paid as well as open source software and what you use depends on what you are most comfortable with.

It may take you some time to develop anything approaching what you think is nice, but it is recommended that you do this yourself if you have the time to spare. It gives you much more control over how you design your own website and you can have everything exactly how you want it.

Follow simple naming conventions

Another reason why it is better for you to develop your own site is that you can follow your own naming convention. Recent studies have showed that sites that have easy to remember addresses tend to get more traffic than those that have a meaningless jumble of numbers and alphabets.

For example if you want to have a website that reviews software, just go with www.thesitename/home. If from there you want to have a page about you, then follow the same principle except that instead of /home you will have /aboutme. This is much better than having something that looks like this www.thesitename/landing/ID=250?/etc/whatnot/somemorenonse nse.

There may be a very good reason for you doing this, but it is better to have things simple. Your address is not a password for it to have alpha numeric characters.

Why this matters is really not known except that it does seem to have an impact on web traffic.

Dominate Your Market Niche

In the same way links that lead deeper into your own website needs to have meaningful keywords, not a link with click here on it. You may think that this is default, but it is very easy to overlook these small things that have a big impact on the numbers.

- **Use the Right Content**

Using the right content is a very important factor when it comes to developing your website. Optimizing the content does not only refer to SEO or Search Engine Optimization, but also to the layout of the website as well as each page.

SEO

This is an acronym that has been used and reused so many times that many people think that this is the only thing about a website that makes it get a higher ranking. Obviously search engines will make use of keywords to index your articles, but the problem is that when writing content we can only take into account a few words or phrases that we think is what the whole world is looking for. Yet, all search engines will pull out your articles even using other keywords, words that you would not consider as keywords at all.

The best thing to do is to use industry specific words to ensure that you have a wide distribution of words. For example, if you are creating a food website where you plan on putting up different recipes, make sure that you include all the words that you think will be used to search for your article. Words like cooking, recipes, dish etc. are all different words that can be used because it is all different ways for the public to search for the same thing.

There is fierce competition with regards to optimizing the content and most of the larger websites would make sure that they corral most if not all the keywords that they think are important. Yet, this does not mean that your site will be low down in the ranking. Ranking of a site by a search engine is based on a combination of factors and SEO is only one of them.

Layout Optimization

Most search engines use programs called spiders or crawlers to index your site. These spiders or crawlers are nothing but programs that mimic human behavior but with the added capacity to tag and index everything that they visit. Generally speaking these crawlers go top to down and left to right. This means that the top left hand corner of your site is the most valuable piece of real estate while the bottom right hand corner is the least.

Knowing this will help you to optimize your layout better. For example if you are designing your home page, it would be a better idea to put in the links to other informational content on top and less important information like the about us link at the bottom.

Always Tag Pictures

Another thing that you should remember is that crawlers cannot read through graphics or scripts. This means that even if you subscribe to the belief that a picture is worth a thousand words, it is still a good idea for you to write a dozen words under the picture defining what it is. Only this text will be used by the search engine for its indexing purposes, which is why if you look up any result in Google images you will sometimes find that the images do not have anything to do with your search string, but the keywords would be present in its description.

Some people use this defect to leverage their site by adding in keywords that are not entirely suitable, and you are the only judge

Dominate Your Market Niche

as to whether this is a risk worth taking. Search engines are always evolving, and if at some point in the future they redefine their algorithm so that they can identify such keyword stuffing, you will find that your website has all of a sudden lost its ranking. Google is definitely not going to notify the world that it is going to do this giving you time to change your site. When you find out it is already too late.

CHAPTER 8- SOME QUICK GUIDELINES ON BLOGGING

Blogging is something that most web surfers do. They either have their own blogs or they comment on others'. Having a blog page where you can post your thoughts and have others respond is therefore a good idea. A blog is not a comments page for your article. A blog is where people can share their thoughts on the articles posted.

You can therefore have a website where you give reviews and sell software, and have a blog where you can discuss everything from how a certain IT company is following trade practices to the state of the economy. These comments may not find suitable space anywhere other than your blog and having a separate page for it is a good idea.

A Blog in Your Site

This is something that a number of people fail to do. They will have a website and have a blog, but they will both be in different domains. Some people actually go to the time and the effort of creating their own website but host their blogs using free software like WordPress

Leaving aside the impracticality of this, you will also be losing out on driving traffic to your site from your blog. Web traffic is not all generated through just one source and it is only by combining a number of sources that you get where you want to be. Blogs are one of these options. If you have started blogging about an interesting topic there is every reason for people to follow through to your website if it were in the same domain. By splitting them up in different locations you are losing on a certain amount of the traffic.

The best way is to host your blog as a sub-domain of your primary domain which is your website, and the worst is to use other hosting sites like BlogSpot or WordPress. By hosting your WordPress blog on your own web space, you increase your website size and content range, by discussing and talking about your website content via your own blog. This way the search engines not only see your website blog, but they also see your website which is linking in. Creating back links to your website from blogs is an amazing way to get extra traffic.

Don't Create Fake Comments, It Shows

Most people who create their websites make sure that they incorporate a comments section. This is done so that people who visit can start to leave comments. This is very useful because many times people who comment on your section will also link back to their articles on similar topics. Of course, people do this to increase their own ranking, but it is also helpful to you if you have more unique people linking to your site. It improves your standing with the search engines tremendously.

There is one problem with this though and that this section is like a two edged sword. If you are a regular web surfer you would have come across umpteen sites where there is not one single comment written. Of course you can employ others to write in a few, but it is very easy to make out the real ones from the fake. Rather than do this it is better to leave the comments section blank.

Yet, leaving it blank seems to imply that your site really does not have many followers. It can give an empty feeling to the site and even if the content is quite good, just because there is not a single comment in it many people will not return to your site.

When do I start it?

The best way to tackle this is to start up this section after some time. During this time you will be trying various different methods to improve the rankings and improve traffic to your site. Once you find that you are getting around 500 to 700 hits that stay for some time every day would be the right time for you to start this section. If you are offering an RSS feed you can start as soon as you hit the one hundred subscribers mark.

What you are ensuring by doing this is that your site has a minimum quorum that will at least follow up on comments once someone starts off. Plus, you are also improving your chances of having at least one in this group who will in the least leave a "Good job" in the comments section. Of course, you may lose out on comments on previous articles, but it is a risk that you will have to take.

There is no rule governing how long it will take for this to happen. For all you know you may start seeing a lot of activity in your blog once you post your first article itself and if you find that there are a number of people leaving comments about what you have written, you can open the section on the second day itself. All we advise you to do is to open the comments section only when you feel that you will have a good number of followers who will use the section instead of leaving it empty.

A Sitemap Is a Necessity

A sitemap is just one page where you have the whole layout of your website. Smaller simpler websites may not necessarily want one, but sites that have a number of pages definitely have to have one. This page is very important for two reasons.

First, if you have or are planning to have a large number of pages to your website, it is better to have one page from where people can navigate to different places on your site. It makes the whole browsing experience simpler making sure that you do not lose any visitors because they feel that navigating your site is too complicated.

Second, this page is important because you can submit this page to search engines to index. This has the double advantage of forcing the search engine crawlers to follow all the links in the page thus indexing all pages and also ensures that your site gets indexed quicker. Sometimes, especially if your site has a large number of pages crawlers do not probe more than two links into the site meaning that pages that lead deeper into your site are left un-indexed.

Many people who have such sitemaps find that this page gets ranked much higher in most search engines for most keywords than the actual page dealing with the keyword giving you the double benefit of a higher ranking as well as making sure that people visit other pages in your site.

How do you organize the sitemap?

This is basically up to you. Some people just have one page where they have links to all the pages in their website. This page will not be visible to the browsing public, but will be useful for the search engines to index all the pages in your website. This is the simplest form of having a sitemap. Others use JavaScript drop down menus to help navigate their sites, but then the crawlers do not read this. This means that you will have to have a text version of the sitemap done just so that it gets indexed. You can always keep this portion invisible while keeping the scripted portion visible.

The formatting of the page is up to you. Depending on the number of main pages you can follow the traditional top across, or left vertical method. If you are good at designing you can even follow a completely new method. It is however safer to stick with the traditional if only because it gives some familiarity to your website from the point of view of first time visitors.

CHAPTER 9- WHEN DOES THE BIG TRAFFIC COME?

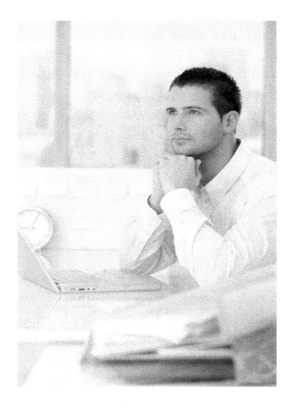

Traffic to websites is a very fickle thing. There may be days when there is almost no activity, and there may be days when the amount of activity can almost bring your site down. Only with experience can you gauge if there is any pattern to this or not. Different sites dealing with different subjects have different patterns and there is no way to gauge what sort of traffic pattern you will have until you start yours and keep it running for some time.

It is however a given that there will be days when you see a bump up in traffic. There may be a very sound reason for this, for example, if you are releasing new software on your site. Other times, your site may be pulled out of near obscurity simply because some factor outside your influence has turned the public eye your way.

For example, if you have a site that deals with global warming, you will see a certain amount of activity on a daily basis, and then one fine day there may be a storm somewhere that put a whole township under water, or a huge chunk of an iceberg may break off the Antarctic. The next day you may see a tremendous jump up in traffic.

As soon as you see that there is a jump in the traffic, even if only slight, make sure that you take advantage of it. Start increasing the number of posts, and make sure that there is some activity in your site within the next 24 hrs. Some web surfers are not known the most loyal and will immediately forget about your site if there is nothing happening for more than a day.

In this day and age where things happen really fast, it is the people who keep track and take advantage of small shifts in traffic patterns who do well. The web is a media outlet much like your television, and if there is something happening and a particular channel is not covering it, how long would you stay with that channel. Exactly how long others will stay with you if you do not take advantage of something happening in your field.

You may only have a site that has software for sale, but if Apple is releasing a new version of their iPod it is best to take it up. If you feel that the topic is outside the scope of your site, start a topic on your blog, that's what blogs are for. This is also a good way of driving traffic to your site, especially if you have your blog as a sub-domain.

Patience Pays Off

There is probably no other piece of advice that is as important as this. It takes time to do anything and there is no way that you are going to become an instant success. If you take the success stories of any person, you will find that there are two things in common, hard work and time.

Do not start a website unless you feel passionately that it will work. If you do believe that it will work you should be willing to sacrifice a lot of time and effort to make it work. Even if you have the best content and do everything else that is supposed to guarantee that your site will become a hit, you still need to give sufficient time for it to work.

Google Sandbox

Another reason for being patient is because of something that is commonly referred to as the Google sandbox. This sandbox is just a theory that a number of web masters feel is true although Google has not come right out and admitted it. A few things that they have mentioned however seem to indicate that there is a sandbox that Google uses.

This sandbox is just a virtual box where Google dumps new websites or sites that Google believes are setting out deliberately to cheat their search engine, or even sites that have been taken over by spammers. Since there is no direct conformation from Google that there is really a sandbox finding out if your website is there is a little difficult.

There are a few pointers though. First, if you have just launched your website, it is almost guaranteed that your site is there. It is possible that your site can have a page rank, and it may even pop up on subsidiary searches, but any direct search will not show your site on the results page.

This sandboxing is different from Google penalizing you. If you are in penalty then you will lose your page rank and sometimes the Google search area may even be greyed out. In the sandbox the website just sits around until Google deems it to be a worthy website to start to display on its results page.

Why This Sandbox?

Since designing web pages is actually not as expensive as other forms of marketing, many organizations started to create websites just for promotional purposes and then shut it down. This meant that there were a number of results with broken links in Google, not a good thing for any search engine.

Spammers are another reason for this. Until this sandboxing by Google started, spammers used to start a site just to send out spam, but these sites tended to get very high ranking in a short time, once again something that search engines do not want in their results.

There are a number of other reasons for Google adopting this policy, but suffice it to say that it is there for a purpose, to weed out the real from the fake. The duration that websites stay in this sandbox can last anywhere between a couple of months to a year. Nobody has too much information about this, and your guess is probably as good as any other person's out there. The only thing that you can do here is to be patient. Continue with adding in more content and link back, in short continue to operate as if your website were not in limbo. There are two reasons for this. One is the very simple reason that Google is not going to notify you before it removes your site from its sandbox and unless you are prepared you will be caught napping.

The other reason is that you can take this time to refine your website so that once it comes out of the sandbox you will be ready to take advantage of an exponential increase in your ranking.

You Can't Beat It

There are a number of websites that offer supposedly guaranteed ways to remove your site from the sandbox, but it is good to take all this advice with a pinch of salt. Google has done this with a purpose and unless you can show specific cause, there is no reason for them to excuse you. Even if you do everything that you can think of to show Google that you are really a genuine site, there is no guarantee that it will work.

It is much better to include this time into your ramping up schedule but have a strategy in place to take advantage of the time that your website comes out of the sandbox.

Of course you can purchase an established site instead of creating one of your own, which means that you can hit the ground running, but even here, people have found that sites that frequently change their ownership find themselves put into the sandbox. It is useless to speculate on why this happens. A much better idea is for you to accept it and plan accordingly.

Be Eternally Nice

This is the final piece of the jigsaw and is both the first as well as the last thing that you have to remember. People sometimes tend to confuse being professional with not being nice without realizing that you can be professional and at the same time be nice.

Jeff Moore

Being nice is not something that you should have to work at. It is supposed to come naturally, as naturally as wishing your neighbors "Good morning". Yet it is still something that you should always keep in mind because with success comes an inflated sense of your own importance, and then you will not be nice any longer.

Why this being nice is important is because if you leave aside the purely moralistic aspect of this, it will tend to net you more money than if you are not. Just think of yourself going out to buy something, would you rather go to a person who is nice to you and makes you feel comfortable, or go to a place that does not. Most times even if going to the store where you like to go takes you longer you will still want to go there.

People online are the same; they will tend to overlook some faults on your side just because you are nice. Over time you can build such a strong brand image that it will become the hallmark of your website and yours can actually be a case in point of how even a very ordinary looking website has still managed to get such a high ranking on Google and manages to consistently hit numbers in the millions every week.

People do not visit a site anymore because it looks nice or because the graphics are amazing. This has become so common that there is nothing new in it. If you do go this way you will have to introduce some change every other week and not only is this exhausting, you will be incurring tremendous costs too.

People come to you because their browsing experience is good, and one of the best ways of doing this is being nice. Respond to every comment that people leave. Thank someone who wishes you well and help out someone who is asking you for it, however inane the question is. There are many ways in which you can be nice that it is practically impossible to tell a person how. It is just in the

Dominate Your Market Niche

mindset. Many people who are nice enough in the beginning tend to get a little abrasive once they see a bit of success without even realizing that they have become so and it is best if you bear this in mind.

Chapter 10 - BONUS! Free Tips on Converting Traffic to Buying Customers

1. Write a Roundup Post

A roundup post is an entry that speaks about a group of people in your niche. This strategy is used to build relationships with influencers in your niche. Let them know that you are reaching out to them and promoting their content. More often than not, this leads to them returning you the favor by blogging or tweeting about you. If they are indeed influential in your niche, their return of favor will be sending massive traffic your way.

2. Interview Experts in Your Niche

If you can get interviews with experts in your niche, your credibility will be greatly boosted thus generating more traffic. All you have to do is ask: email experts a list of questions that is relevant to your niche and get some great content from their answers. At the same time, build relationships with these experts because you never know when a powerful partnership will come knocking at your door.

3. Twitter Traffic.

Twitter can be a huge source of traffic for you if you know how to build your Twitter network on a daily basis. Your goal with Twitter is to network and build relationships and these relationships can lead to more traffic. One Twitter post can become so viral that it can send tens of thousands of visitors to your sites if done in the right manner.

4. Create a Facebook Page

Studies have shown that people are spending more time on Facebook than any other website on the internet. By being in front of such traffic, you have the best chance of being seen on the vast web. Create a Facebook Page for your website and install a "Like Box" into your website so that your visitors will know you are on Facebook and join as a fan on your Facebook Page.

5. Create an Infographic

If you are great with design, you can take the statistics of any topic and create an infographic to represent the figures. Infographics can go viral very easily as people like to share them all over the web. Do remember to include your website URL within the infographic so that you can get the traffic when it is re-blogged elsewhere on the internet. You know what? Forget about being great with design, you can outsource it to someone else to get it done for you!

6. Create a .pdf Cheat sheet

Create cheat sheets with important information about a certain topic and include your website URLs where possible inside the document. People love content such as this and there is a very good chance that it will go viral being shared on the web.

7. Create a Memorable Domain

Domain names often give people a first impression of the website. A good domain will attract the massive amounts of traffic. The most effective domains are the .com domains.

8. Produce Videos on YouTube

One of the largest search engines other than Google is none other than YouTube. Therefore, it is crucial to include YouTube in your arsenal of traffic strategies. Create your own YouTube channel. Produce and upload original videos with interesting content to your YouTube channel. Using the "annotation" feature while editing YouTube videos, you can add a call to action for viewers to go your website URL. Another strategy is to interlink your videos with annotations so as to pick up more views and more traffic. Optimize your YouTube channel by including a link back to your website in the profile information on the left panel. Here's an excellent YouTube course: Video Traffic Academy

9. Optimize your YouTube videos with searchable keywords

After producing and uploading interesting video content to YouTube, optimize your YouTube videos by tagging your video with searchable keywords. For phrases, remember to include the quotation punctuation:" "

10. Screencast Videos

Creating screencast videos is an effective way you can use to drive traffic to you website. One strategy is to attach a screencast near the end of the video to persuade visitors to check out your website. Talk about it for short while, pointing out the cool things visitors can find on your website. Some software I would recommend is Camtasia or Jing.

11. Write Guest Posts

Many bloggers or webmasters have audiences to their websites amounting more than your own. Approach these people and ask them if they would like for you to write a post for their blog. Not only will you possibly get traffic flocking to your site, it will also get you quality backlinks that will boost the ranking of your site on Google. In addition, you would have made a friend or friends and build relationships in the process.

12. Create an Ecourse

An easy yet effective way to start your email series is by offering a 5-day / 7-day email course where you send emails automatically for the next 5/7 days to build a strong relationship and trust with your subscribers. Include links in your email for them to revisit your website. Once you have built a substantial list of raving subscribers, you will be able to create a sustainable amount of traffic that is going to your website.

13. Hold a Contest for Subscribers

Organize contests where you give away prizes to winners. You can do this as a one-time only or monthly contest. The bigger your gift, the more buzz you generate online and hence the more traffic to

Jeff Moore

your site from those who sign up. Here's an excellent contest script: Contest Burner

14. Retweet Contest

If you are active on Twitter, you might have seen some of the marketing tactics in Twitter campaigns. One idea is that you could hold a contest to make the entry based on tweeting a certain link. Using backtweets, you can track those who have tweeted your link.

15. Content Contest

Ever finding it hard to write content? You can hold a Content Contest where you ask users to answer a question to enter a contest and the best answer wins a prize. Not only will you get a massive amounts of traffic because the contest prizes attracts people, when the contest is finished you should have a healthy article filled with insightful responses to any question you want.

16. Traffic Contest

An easy way to effectively get your website ranked and found on search engines is to hold a SEO contest where the person who sent the most traffic to the contest page wins an awesome prize. This can be done is by each user having their own bit.ly URL. All bit.ly URLs have built in analytics that can be accessed by adding a + to the end of the link.

17. Make your blog available on Kindle

The Amazon Kindle is an e-book reader which uses wireless connectivity to enable users to shop for, download, browse, and read e-books, newspapers, magazines, blogs, and other digital media. With more than 54 million hits a month, Amazon is the ultimate traffic-driver; even if you never own a Kindle you should make your blog available on Kindle as it will position you as an authority in your field.

18. Install the Alexa toolbar on your browser

The Alexa Toolbar is a Firefox extension that is used by Alexa to measure website specific statistics. It is crucial to install the Alexa toolbar because Goggle uses Alexa's Information for ranking and indexing. After installing the toolbar, surfing your own site will absolutely help you get your sites indexed by Google more quickly.

19. Install Social Sharing Plugins

Install social sharing plugins like Facebook and Twitter sharing buttons. Share this is one service that offers you to share content on Facebook and Twitter and other content hubs. Always add links to your Twitter updates and use other pages other than your Home page, like your About page, as a landing page. This is helping you to gather more traffic to your site.

20. Take advantage of Mobile Traffic

With the increasing number of smart phone users around the world, you should take advantage of the amounts of mobile traffic by optimizing your content for mobile.

21. Add your Site to Directories

Most directories offer the free option to add your URL to their listings. You will be able to pick up some high quality backlinks by adding your site to directories. This is to get your site ranking well on Google.

22. Add your Blog to Blog Directories

Blog-only directories will get you more link juice and traffic from people who are browsing the directory. So, do add your blog URL to blog directories to increase your site exposure.

23. Build Links with Other Web Masters

Another effective way to get more traffic is to put your website link on another website related to your niche. Most webmasters don't mind doing a link exchange with you if you are to provide a reciprocal link on your site as well. In this way, Google sees the links as two way links. However, one way links are perceived to be more powerful than two way links. Therefore if you have two sites, build links with other bloggers by linking them with one site and having them link to the other. This way you and the blogger both get one way links. If you have three or more blogs you can apply this same strategy internally.

24. Do Ad Swaps with Other People in Your Niche

Cross promote by doing ad swaps with someone in your niche to get more traffic and build a substantial email list. Firstly, find someone in your niche with a similar sized email list. Send an email about their opt-in offer to your list, and they will reciprocate by sending an email about your opt-in offer to their list.

25. Submit Press Releases

A press release is a written or recorded communication directed at members of the news media for the purpose of announcing something newsworthy. They may be an old school technique, but press releases still work. Here's excellent software that will help you with your PR submission: Press Equalizer

26. Conduct Proper Keyword Research

Keyword research help you to find relevant keywords that are high in demand but low in level competition. Use the Google Keyword tool to gather this information and then use it for search engine optimization or cost per click campaigns to get your website ranked to be found my prospective customers. Or you could use awesome Keyword Research software like: Micro Niche Finder

27. Start a Podcast

Start a Podcast to get your content out to the millions of people with iPods and other Apple products. It allows you to build up an audience who you can form strong relationships with. You can learn more about podcasting here: Niche Podcasting

28. Link to your site in your Email Signature

You can get traffic to your site with every email you send. Therefore, set up a custom signature with a link to your website. In addition, have it as an anchor text with the title of your site, because in that way, there is a good chance that it will get clicked.

29. Customize your 404 error page

Suggest other content on your site to visitors with a custom designed 404 page. This is so that even if they accidentally land on that page, they don't bounce from your site.

30. Solo Ads

Find a reputable list owner who guarantees a certain amount of clicks and work out a deal for the list owner to mail a list for you for a payment. This is list building technique you can use to generate more traffic to your site.

31. Speed up your Website

When we talk about the internet, we are always talking about speed. When a website takes more than a few seconds to load some visitors will leave simply because they are impatient. Therefore speed up your website. This can be done by compressing your images or installing a w3 cache plugin to your WordPress site.

32. Get Quality Website Hosting

Even if you can generate a lot of traffic to your website, your traffic might not have a site to visit if your website can't show because your website hosting is of low quality. Go with a host that is well established and has great customer service.

33. Add a translation widget to your site

Install a translation widget to your site if you want non-English traffic to your site. One such tool can be the Google Translate Tool.

34. Submit your Site to Search Engines

Manually submit your new site to Google, Yahoo and BING to inform that to crawl it on a regular basis. For a WordPress blog, install the Google XML Sitemaps plugin to enable crawling spiders to check out your site regularly.

35. Comment on other blogs

Mashable and TechCrunch are big blogs where many people visit to read stuff. Be the first to comment on their posts for maximum visibility.

36. Spy on Your Competitors Links

Find your biggest competitors by searching for your keywords in Google. Take the top results from there and spy on their backlinks. Copy your competitor's URL and paste it in the yahoo search bar in this manner: link:pageurl -site:domain.com This will show you the links that are pointing to this page so that you can attempt to duplicate them.

ABOUT THE AUTHOR

Jeff Moore is an internet marketer. He is the brains behind several successful marketing campaigns; thus making him an authority when it comes to increasing website traffic.

Jeff holds webinars to impart his valuable knowledge to others and help them succeed.

www.ingramcontent.com/pod-product-compliance
Lightning Source LLC
Chambersburg PA
CBHW070859070326
40690CB00009B/1910